The Contemplative
in the World

Mother Mary Clare SLG

SLG Press
Convent of the Incarnation
Fairacres Oxford

Second Impression 1992

ISBN 0 7283 0116 4
ISSN 0307-1405

Preface

To celebrate the publication of Fairacres Publication No. 100, the Press is adding to its list this pamphlet which is made up of talks given by Mother Mary Clare to members of our Fellowship of the Love of God. We believe it will be of value to others who are also called to live the contemplative life in the world.

Monastic spirituality is open to all. This paragraph from the Rule of the SLG Oblates would speak to many people today.

> Christians are called to follow our Lord's example and his charge to his disciples—to be in the world, not to be conformed to it but to serve it. This service involves a judgment of affairs and situations from the Christian standpoint in order to help men to recognize and accept those insights of truth to which Christians witness.

Increasing numbers of people are discovering that, to quote from a later passage in the same Rule:

> Prayer is possible in all circumstances . . . Contemplatives are called to take part in the underlying spiritual conflict, and to bring the healing power of Christ into every situation.

This call to the contemplative life may explain why increasing numbers of people who are not actually called to become religious find fulfilment in an association with a religious community. The link may be a formal one, as in the case of Oblates, Tertiaries, or Associates; or it may be informal—simply going as a friend of the community for long or short visits.

About thirty years ago, not long after Mother Mary Clare had become Mother, the Community bought Nos. 38 and 44 Fairacres Road; and in 1959, for the first time, a group of members of the Fellowship came to stay for a retreat. Looking back on the event, one can see that her vision of the vocation of the contemplative in the world, and therefore, what she taught, about the relationship of the Christian life in the world, and our life in community, was prophetic.

Fellowship House is so named because its primary purpose is to be available to members of the Fellowship and Companions.

It also enables us to offer hospitality to a limited number of other visitors who come to learn about the community, to spend a few days in retreat and to share our silence, or to be with a member of their family. When we first acquired the house the neighbours were, I believe, apprehensive about having what they expected to be a 'dead' house next door. I do not think they would now use that term to describe No. 38, which is constantly in use—nor would we so describe the hidden work of those who come.

The Fellowship is made up of a wide variety of people living in the world who have found themselves called to a life of prayer and discipline appropriate to their circumstances, and who have found their association with the community a source of inspiration and encouragement. We in our turn, find our contact with them an enrichment and an important part of our work and prayer.

As you will notice from the photographs of Fellowship House on the cover, the path leading from the Visitors' Chapel leads to the gate that opens on to Fairacres Road. This speaks to me of the mission of the contemplatives living in the world to offer their life of prayer in the ordinary circumstances where this work is vital. As Mother Mary Clare says,

> . . . you draw from the community's ordered life of worship and enclosure. But you draw from us in order to be enkindled and refuelled to give your own essential contribution of worship and of sacrifical living in the world where God has placed you.

The gate through which our visitors pass is also an apt symbol of the reciprocal exchange, in pursuit of a common goal, between those called to live prayer and pray life in this or any convent or monastery, and those called to do the same outside it.

MOTHER JANE SLG

I AM GOING to say things which some of you will know as well as I do about the relationship of your Christian life in the world to our life in the Community of the Sisters of the Love of God, but there are some of you whose first contact it is with the community as a praying body. First of all, let us be deeply thankful for Fellowship House since it makes possible this gathering and your continuous participation in the worship and offering of the community at Mass and in the Divine Office. Earlier retreats with Father Cary SSJE at St Thomas's Convent were channels through which he could and did teach and train his spiritual children, but it has not been possible until now for retreatants to come and stay under the shadow of the convent roof.

The real point of why you have come is to take your part as praying members of the community. The aim of this weekend is to deepen our awareness of the vocation to the contemplative life and to contemplative prayer. Both the contemplative life and contemplative prayer are the fruits of sensitiveness to the Spirit's promptings. I believe that as your spirits become increasingly attuned to the rhythm of the community worship and as you take your full share in the corporate prayer of the Church, you will know more of and desire increasingly to share in the worship and sacrificial offering to which the community is pledged. As we all know, it is not merely a question of rule or of times of prayer—some of you can give only a quarter of an hour, others an hour and a half daily—but rather it is the spirit in which you live your life that is of primary importance. You need, therefore, to know something more of the spirit and life of the community and also to have a lively sense of the part that you and we play in the mainstream of the Church's life.

THE GREAT TRADITION

I am sure there is need to stimulate the contemplative dedications in the world today. These vocations are real outposts of the contemplative communities. Bodies of tertiaries, oblates, or associates of enclosed communities can be and should be centres of witness to those supernatural and eternal principles for which the contemplative life stands. The inmost heart of a contemplative offering is of spirit, not of place, so your offering is to be a deeply interior and hidden one, maintained and offered very often in the midst of great claims and outward activity. Here you will appreciate the relevance of the following passage from *The Lord of History* by Jean Daniélou:

> the old Christian world, or worldly Christianity, is breaking up under the irresistible pressure of new and vital forces . . . this furnishes the explanation of a development which I take to be peculiarly characteristic of our own time, namely the re-entry of contemplatives into the active life of the world. For in the early days of Christianity, the holy virgins and the men of prayer lived their daily lives as part of the one Christian community in full contact with the world of paganism. The flight into the desert was a revolutionary innovation, dating from the fourth century, when St Anthony inaugurated the age of monks, the withdrawal of the contemplatives from a world in which Christianity was compromised, into the solitudes where they might keep alive the faith of the martyrs. That age is passing—St Anthony is coming back from his desert; there is no need for flight now that the Church is once again an army of martyrs, in the midst of a heathen society. 'My factory is my desert.' (p. 77)

Your factory is your desert. It is for that reason that you rightly look to us for the strength and support you draw from the community's ordered life of worship and enclosure. But you draw from us in order to be enkindled and refuelled to give your own essential contribution of worship and of sacrificial living in the world where God has placed you.

What do we mean when we speak of the contemplative life? Father Cary used to quote these words in illustration:

> The activity of the contemplative must be born of his contemplation and must resemble it. Everything he does outside his contemplation ought to reflect the burning tranquillity of his interior life. It is above all in the silent witness and unconscious testimony to the love of God that the contemplative exercises his apostolate, for he preaches sermons by the way he walks, the way he stands, the way he sits down, the way he picks things up and holds them in his hands, and by the reverence with which he makes his whole life an offering of worship to God.

In other words, a wholly God-centred life becomes the channel through which the love and light and life of God can be and *is* radiated forth. Father Cary's ideal of reparation was a life so purified, so God-centred that it becomes a mirror in which the face of God can be seen and can be reflected. A high ideal, yes, but not an impossible one. It is an ideal to grow into, to hope for and to aspire after.

If our mutual offering of prayer and of worship is to be as rich as it could be, we must all see our share in the contemplative life of the Church in its right historical perspective. Even many years after its rebirth, the contemplative life in the Anglican Communion is still in an experimental stage, and we are seeking, indeed the whole Western Church is seeking in the face of the worldwide upheaval of the twentieth century, the rediscovery of what Dom Butler in *Western Mysticism*, calls the recovery of the great tradition in prayer. We are seeking to rediscover this tradition in order to develop our own.

As I see it, it means gaining knowledge from the common ground of the early Fathers, both Eastern and Western, from Cassian to St Augustine, and from the great medieval masters of the spiritual life, including St Bernard, but with special emphasis on the English school of mystics with its stress on affective prayer as introduced by Julian of Norwich, by Walter Hilton, and the writings of the author of *The Cloud of Unknowing*, right on to Augustine Baker. This tradition will lead us on and up into the spiritual experience of the Jesus prayer.

Here we have the common ground of our own SLG prayer spirit and tradition, for we would historically then go straight to the Carmelites as exponents of that same great tradition. You know that Father Cary did not base our Rule on an exact copy of any of the ancient orders of the West, but he did draw extensively on the spirituality of the great leaders of the Carmelite Reform, St Teresa herself and St John of the Cross.

We should also read with due thankfulness and appreciation books by contemporary writers.* In the field of Biblical study and research and its interpretation there are works by Lionel Thornton CR, Austin Farrer, Eric Mascall; in ascetic theology

* See the Suggestions for Further Reading, p. 22

those of F.P. Harton; and on prayer and the spiritual life, the works of Shirley Hughson OHC, Geoffrey Northcott CR, and Father Gilbert Shaw and his books on affective prayer. We can look to all these both for information and right guidance, and the Holy Spirit will lead us, through them, to deepen our individual and corporate response.

THE GLORY OF GOD

This historical perspective must serve as a background to our more detailed consideration and understanding of the aim and spirit of the community. You will probably find that the two words which will recur constantly in my talks are *unity* and *glory*, for it is the work of the Church to incorporate men and women into the life of God incarnate, so that the unity in the community may be an instrument of unity for the Church; and the unity of the Church is drawn from the unity in the Holy Trinity, Three Persons, One God, to whom be glory for ever and ever. Of course we can do nothing of ourselves, but in the power of the risen Christ the influence of a wholly dedicated life is incalculable.

The chapter of our Rule on the aim of the community states clearly: 'The Community of the Sisters of the Love of God has for its aim the glory of God.' Let us think of that glory. There is an immense richness to be discovered in this word *glory* and it concerns the whole of our life. We could, of course, trace this thought through the Old Testament, but for our purpose today, it is the thought of Jesus, the Lord of glory, the revelation of the Father's glory that concerns us, for *he is the way to the Father and the door into this exploration into God.*

When we read the accounts of the first preaching of the apostles in Acts and in the epistles, we must always be struck by the fact that they say so little about the details of our Lord's incarnate life; all the burden of their teaching is that he is the Lord of glory. As Father Cary says:

> The converting message that swept people off their feet was the message that the crucified was the Lord of glory. The sweeping devastating revelation of what he was came first. He, the humble carpenter of Nazareth, he the lover of little children, he the healer of the sick, the teacher—he was Lord of glory and now as God and man he reigns.

4

We are to look through the more homely aspects of the Incarnation to see the wonder of the revelation of pure Godhead, the glory of God shining with undimmed splendour and beauty behind the lowly form of the babe, the teacher, the healer, and the sufferer on Calvary. Not only must we pass through these outward forms and signs into the realization of the reality behind, but we must stay there and allow the glory to pervade our life so that we shall be charged with the life of God and ourselves be reflectors of the glory upon which we gaze.

We all know the story of the refiner of gold. He stokes up his fire and the cauldron boils, the impurities in the gold rise to the surface and he skims them off. Meanwhile the fire has died down, he blows it up again and again the metal boils, the impurities rise and are skimmed off, and so the process goes on until finally there are no impurities to rise and the refiner can see his own face reflected in the pure metal. If we think of our Lord as the refiner and ourselves as the metal in the cauldron of his love, we shall see that as we submit to God's purifying there will come a point in our life when he, the Lord of glory, will see the reflection of his face in us, and so seeing, the travail of his soul will be satisfied. The life of purification here and now is the chief way by which we give him glory: this is what gives us the real motive for our growing penitence in our prayer and sacramental confessions.

If we desire to live the contemplative life, coming through prayer to vision, then we must have consciously in our intention the offered life of sacrifice, that is, reparation under penance for the sin of the world. Contemplation and reparation must go hand in hand. As we grow in the love of God in prayer, so he unfolds to us more and more of his intention for all the world, and as we grow nearer to God, we must grow in the knowledge of God's love for creation and in fuller understanding of the mind of Christ. If God has given us this call then as we see more of our Lord's purpose of divine love, we must long for grace to further that purpose of redeeming love. As we see the sorrows and perversions and distortions that spring from alienation from God, we must realize that the only way to heal those sorrows is to bring them within the scope of the divine love and mercy, to

5

set free the divine life within the souls of men. We believe that it is this spiritual approach which is needed, and this can only be accomplished in that same spirit of sacrifice which animated Jesus. The outward touch, even at best, can only be the longer way of approach to God.

The whole life, if it is true, must be one of discipline and self-abnegation. It does not consist of a series of spiritual poses or self-conscious emotional dreaming or sentimental prayer which does not touch the real life, but it must be disciplined in every part. There is any amount of romance in it, but the work itself is discipline, penance and sacrifice in union with the offered life of our divine Saviour.

If this offering is to enter into the whole of our life, that will include our consecrated use of material things. All things are to be sacramental; we must recognize the divine underneath and use everything as a means of setting free the divine life within us. Our blessed Lord had to use and to come in contact with created things continually. He did not despise them. He used food and clothing, occasions of social intercourse, and in the using he consecrated them all. Those set apart for God, whether vowed to God for ever in the community, or dedicated to him in the Fellowship must in union with our Lord use all things sacramentally. We must remember that in daily life all things that we handle must be used reverently and quietly. All roughness is a form of sacrilege, the misuse of something offered to God. By our careful use of all that God gives us we can make reparation for all the sins of misuse and carelessness among those who have ignored or forgotten the claim of God on their lives. We must not get narrow or scrupulous about the things God gives us to use, but it is to be a disciplined use. As we grow in the spirit of sacrificial love, we become more simple, scruples vanish and the life and love of God himself pour into our hearts to be poured out again on behalf of the world for which our Lord died.

PRAYER WITHIN THE VERTICAL

You have received the call from God to live the contemplative life in the world, and part of that sense of vocation has been to lead you to associate yourselves with the community. You may recall the old analogy of the relation of the vertical, that is, man's relation to God, and that of the horizontal, that is, man's relation to creation. Father Cary used the transverse arms of the Cross to illustrate these aspects of our life. First, let us think about the offering of prayer within the vertical, through the Mass, the Divine Office, and in our private prayer.

About the Mass, I think I need only say that I know that if it is humanly possible you will find yourselves morning by morning at the altar of God, where our great high priest through the blessed sacrament of his body and blood unites his Church on earth to his offering in heaven. In the Mass the members of his body are united to himself, that they too may be strengthened to offer themselves a sacrifice of love and reparation to the heavenly Father for the needs of the whole world. The contemplative should, I am sure, derive special strength and support in the Mass through union with the Church Triumphant in the mystical body.

The holy sacrifice of the Mass and communion is the supreme act of worship, and flowing out from this is the offering of the Divine Office, a work so important that we are bidden as a community to remember that its recitation is not only a fundamental duty but also a privilege of great value.

The perfect prayer of our Lord did not cease when he ascended into heaven. Through his indwelling in his mystical body the Church, it has risen to God unceasingly through the ages. Because of our incorporation in his risen life, our Divine Office is part of the great work of the extension of the Incarnation. When we come to the Divine Office with reverence and recollection it is taken up into the very life of the blessed Trinity.

It is called the Divine Office because it relates wholly to God. The words of holy scripture make up the greater part of the Office: there are the psalms; there are antiphons introducing the psalms, most of which are drawn from some part of scripture; and the hymns and lessons are based on scripture or scriptural ideas. So it is *divine in origin.*

It is divine because it is taken from the lips of the Incarnate Word himself. Our Lord prayed the same psalms and texts from the Old Testament. The present arrangement of the psalms in the Office dates from the Benedictine Office of the sixth century; but the psalms were, of course, recited hundreds of years before

7

by the Jewish people. This wonderful continuity linking our worship through the ages emphasizes strongly its divine origin.

It is *divine in its intention*, because directed to God. The foundation and background of all our recitation of the Office must be the pure worship and homage paid to God.

It is *divine in its enabling*, that is, in the way in which the Holy Spirit enables us to speak and to praise God. By the power of the Holy Spirit we are lifted out of the narrowness of our natural intentions, and the Word of God utters himself again to the Father through the medium of our lips. That is why we say at the beginning, 'O Lord, make haste to help me.' It would be utterly impossible for us to offer such praise worthily by our natural power. Our worthiness must depend upon how we respond to this enabling of the Holy Spirit. This is why our whole life must be purified.

I know many of you in your own prayer rule have the recitation of the Divine Office whole or in part as one of the requirements, and that it is your delight as far as the conditions of your life admit, to join in this corporate prayer of the Church. But I am equally sure that the conditions of modern life demand that you should look at this realistically. What I have said with regard to the canonical Divine Office would apply equally to those who say Mattins and Evensong instead.

Here at the Convent we sing Matins, the Night Office, at 2 a.m. We are granted the privilege of enclosure so that nothing can hinder our recitation of the Office, but some of you will have obligations that conflict with your rule for the saying of Office. You must not get over-burdened by this. I am not preaching laziness, nor am I minimizing the importance of the obligation to keep your rule, but I am saying that there are times when the transmutation of this duty is a real necessity and then you should have no scruples. There are several ways by which under these circumstances you can rightly fulfil your duty:

1. You can unite your intention with the prayer of the community, and by saying an Our Father, unite yourself in spirit with us.

2. You can recite the opening versicles of the Office ('O God make speed to save me.') with the Gloria and the Lesser Litany ('Lord have mercy. Christ have mercy. Lord have

mercy.') and an Our Father, again with the intention with which you would have said the whole Office had you been able to do so.

3. You can unite yourself with that aspect of the Lord's Passion which the Office commemorates, using an aspiration such as 'O Saviour of the world, who by thy Cross and Passion has redeemed us, save us and help us we humbly beseech thee.' This loving intention is a real act of glory and praise to God and one which will sanctify and make fruitful the duties which on this occasion have taken the place of the Office.

Offering specific intentions is not compulsory, each Office in the daily cycle of prayer is in itself an offering of worship for all the intentions of the divine purpose. But for those for whom more detailed intentions are a help, I will give a table to show how the Office, the commemoration of the Passion, and the intercessory activity may be united if so desired.

OFFICE	MYSTERY OF THE PASSION	INTENTION
Matins	Gethsemane and Betrayal	The sin of the night hours; those in danger, the sick, the dying, suicides.
Lauds	Peter's Denial, the Mocking and Handing Over	The world at the beginning of a new day; the Community, the Fellowship.
Terce	The Holy Spirit	The Church and its needs; for vocations to missionary work and to the priesthood.
Sext	The Nailing to the Cross	Mid-day, the height of the world's needs and activities.
None	The Piercing of the Side	The sick and suffering; those who live to relieve pain, doctors, nurses; the reunion of Christendom.
Vespers	Deposition from the Cross	Sanctification of family life; broken homes, children's work, teachers, Christian education.
Compline	The Holy Sepulchre	The departed, especially those who die spiritually uncared for.

I can only speak in very general terms about the prayer rule of contemplatives in the world, as it clearly must be an individual matter for each one under the guidance of the Holy Spirit. Those seeking to grow in the hidden life of prayer should have a special devotion to the Third Person of the Holy Trinity, for it is by his hidden operation in the soul that the life of union will develop and the human spirit be sanctified and made sensitive to his touch.

Prayer is not a matter of words or holy thoughts: it is the growth of a personal relationship between ourselves and God, and it is an ascending scale of experience. It is the very breath of the soul by which it comes alive in union with God. By prayer one is recovered from the isolation with which one has been surrounded by reason of disobedience. This must be the starting point of our real prayer: we must come to God as petitioners, in the humility of our penitence, for we have all sinned and come short of the glory of God. But because we 'have an Advocate with the Father, Jesus Christ the righteous; and he is the propitiation for our sins', and because we are incorporated into his saving life, Christian prayer is inspired not only by penitence and desire but also by adoration and thanksgiving. These two elements must always be present, whatever form our prayer may take. The basis of our spiritual life must be the gift of faith by which we reaffirm our re-creation in Christ; and it is in the body of Christ that we will receive the illumination of the Spirit.

The aim of all our prayer will be the contemplation of God and the things of God, so that we will be led to an increasing depth of understanding and responsiveness to the love that first loved us. Prayer implies our attention being fixed on God, our attention and our will. Surrender must follow attention to make our prayer a reality, and we must give ourselves to God that he may do what he wills with us—which is quite a different thing from our willing what we think ought to be done. This point is especially important when we come to consider the question of intercession.

Through the work of purification, whether by our own self-

10

discipline or by the direct action of God, the will is restored to liberty in Christ so that the Christian may, by dependence on God's grace, recover the freedom both to know and to live in the will of God. 'Where the Spirit of the Lord is, there is liberty', and the hallmark of true prayer is our increasing sensitiveness to the prompting of the Holy Spirit so that we can quickly see and recognize what is the will of God, and rise up with alacrity to respond and to work with it (cf. II Cor 3.17—18). Prayer at its truest and most exacting is letting our Lord's prayer and will have the fullest expression in us.

A word may be said here about the prayer itself. First, our meditation, that *act* of contemplation which is distinct from the *gift* of contemplation or infused prayer which is God's to give or to withhold, will focus our attention on our Lord in some aspect of his incarnate life, perhaps more especially for us in our work of reparation, in his holy Passion. I am not here thinking of the technique of meditation: that will vary according to the prayer of each one, and there are books to tell us of the techniques. I am referring especially to that loving, adoring attention, which is the result of our union with our Lord through the sacramental grace and life of the Church. It is also the result of the knowledge and leading of the Holy Spirit gained in our prayerful reading and study of scripture which makes its contribution and ensures the fruitful use of our prayer hours.

From this attention, this contemplation of him who is the way to the Father, the heart may well be moved to form *affective acts*. Affective acts, occurring during two stages of our growth in prayer, may be of two kinds. In the first stage they may be short phrases that will sum up the exercise of discursive thought which has been part of our meditation, so that these phrases become part of our prayer, a 'talking to God' in contrast to the reasoning that has gone before. These acts are really important, for without them meditation can become little more than an intellectual exercise, valuable as a study but not as a positive offering of devotion. In these acts, or rather by these acts, we give expression to what we have drawn from our meditation. It has been said, 'In meditation we seek, in the affective acts we find and rejoice!' However, these acts spring— by the grace of God—from our own natural senses which must be purified. When the purification of these senses, and later, the purification of the spirit begins, we should not be surprised if we find these avenues of approach to God are closed to us.

In our prayer during the second stage we now find no feeling to stir the heart so that it responds in any way to the truth it contemplates, and so affective prayer becomes an *act of faith*, a real weaning from our own activity so that the supernatural gifts of faith, hope and love may grow in us and the gifts of the Spirit may lead us to a more directly God-centred activity. We must, indeed, in the darkness of faith continue in our acts, otherwise we are likely to fall into discouragement, and it is here that our reading and study of the scriptures is such a necessary background to our prayer. The Liturgy and holy scripture will provide the material in the mind which the Holy Spirit will make use of, and to which he alone can impart reality and understanding. It is the Holy Spirit who illuminates the understanding, and the prayer in this second stage becomes guided by him rather than being laboriously sought out by us and maintained by the energy of our will.

Then as our natural senses are closed down, as it were, by the night of the senses, affective prayer receives a new spontaneity, and now it is more truly the Spirit of God which maketh intercession in us, and it is he who holds the soul in its contemplation of the things of God. So our affective prayer grows in simplicity as it increases, and becomes more quiet; and just a single word will be sufficient to hold the attention to God. As the author of *The Cloud of Unknowing* tells us:

> lift up thine heart unto God with a meek stirring of love . . . And if thou desirest to have this intent lapped and folden in one word, so that thou mayest have better hold thereupon, take thee but a little word of one syllable, for so it is better than of two; for the shorter the word, the better it accordeth with the work of the spirit. And such a word is this word God or this word Love. Choose whichever thou wilt, or another: whatever word thou likest best of one syllable. And fasten this word to thine heart, so that it may never go thence for anything that befalleth. This word shall be thy shield and thy spear, whether thou ridest on peace or on war. With this word, thou shalt beat on this cloud and this darkness above thee. With this word, thou shalt smite down all manner of thought under the *cloud of forgetting*. (ch. 7, ed. McCann)

That 'little word', which is a quieter form of prayer, may lead us on to the point where the spirit is stilled and the will is united to God. Then there may come a moment when the Spirit of God steps in and takes over control, and without knowing it we have passed into that realm of contemplative prayer where the Spirit will do all. This is a pure gift of God, and we cannot of ourselves attain to it, but we can prepare the way by purification, by faithful perseverance in the other forms of prayer. In contemplative prayer time and eternity meet—'there was silence in heaven about the space of half an hour'.

I need hardly say that none of our activity of prayer, either corporate or personal, will be what God desires it to be unless we are growing in the spirit of *recollection*. Recollection is a gift of the Spirit, but it does need to be cultivated, and we must be humble and patient and build up the habit. The chapter on Silence of our Rule gives guidance on the development of this spirit of recollection:

> It is in silence that the spirit will be trained to deepen recollection and to exercise itself after the likeness of the Seraphim and Cherubim that worship round the throne of God. But it should be remembered that silence must cover all the levels of the conscious life; there must be an outward silence of speech and movement, a silence of the mind for the overcoming of vain imaginations and distractions and a silence of the soul in the surrender of the will to be still and know that God is God, leading to a silence of spirit which is the preparation for the fullness of contemplation.

Be watchful! How do you use those moments when your attention is not actively employed as you walk in the streets or travel in trains and buses, or fulfil some purely routine domestic work? These are the times when the thought should be trained to go Godward on the vertical, or outward on the horizontal for some intercessory need, or to renew interiorly the intention and offering of the morning's Communion. It is in these humble ways that recollection is established. Recollection, which is the foundation of learning to pray always, is developed through learning to pray, not with a multiplicity of thought, but with the simplicity of great love.

Let us try to share some thoughts on the subject of reparation and of our intercessory activity as part of the work of love. Prayer on the horizontal is the overflow of love from the vertical to the horizontal. It is not an easy subject to talk about, and is something which one can only learn by experience. What is this work? Surely it is the fruit of the Passion in our souls. It is not our own activity, but the power of the Cross in our lives. It brings to mind the passage from John Donne:

> No man is an *Iland*, intire of it selfe; every man is a peece of the *Continent*, a part of the *maine*, if a *Clod* bee washed away by the *Sea*, *Europe* is the lesse, as well as if a *Promontorie* were, as well as if a *Mannor* of thy *friends* or of *thine owne* were; any mans *death* diminishes *me*, because I am involved in *Mankinde*; And therefore never send to know for whom the *bell* tolls; It tolls for *thee*. . . .

That is a tremendous truth and a very staggering one if we really contemplate it and think of its implication. The whole subject of reparation and intercession rests on this unity and solidarity of mankind. We are affected by the interaction of personalities and events, and even our thoughts can influence one another. Since 'No man is an Iland', we cannot be surprised if we share and ourselves feel the impetus of the world's tension. How can our prayer affect the situation? We must try to bring the peace of God into the tension and distortion of the world by deepening our own union with God so that *his* peace, the peace of the Son of God, may flow out through us into the darkness.

Think of the lighthouse which stands out in the ocean. The waves and storms beat upon it, yet the light shines out—but remember that it is not the lighthouse that gives the light, the light shines through a lantern. Our vocation is to be a lighthouse which holds the lantern, through which the light of God can stream out: putting love in where love is not, unity where there is disunity, peace where there is fear and suspicion. The contemplatives in the world, whether singly or in groups, provide the Church's lighthouses dedicated to reflect the light of the glory of God in the face of Jesus Christ.

Let me quote from Father Cary to show how the vocation to

a life of reparation is a vocation to seek *holiness*, with the clear intention of sharing in our Lord's work of reconciliation:

> Press after that vision which leaves no room in your heart for anything else. From that purity of light and love reflected from God in you, there will flow through you strength for the stricken world. That to me is the only reparation worthy of being offered to Almighty God. It is the principle of spiritual radiation—holiness by which we give back to God that love, that oneness of will that has been destroyed by the sin and selfhood of mankind. Remember that it is always in and through Jesus Christ our Lord and there is no other way. 'Put ye on the Lord Jesus Christ' and by his action in you, his life in your soul, by the divine invasion of your whole being you will be offering that reparation most dear to God.

Reparation in our Lord's life meant: 'I have no will but thine', 'Father, if thou be willing, remove this cup from me: nevertheless not my will, but thine be done.' The Son glorified the Father by the perfect obedience of his suffering love of which the Cross is the shining example. We must be prepared to be with him on the way to Calvary, following his footsteps in whatever way the divine will may come to us. We were redeemed, as Father Cary so often reminded us, not by the sufferings of Jesus, but by the love of which his sufferings were the expression. Love rightly may prefer hard things, and we must all, in our measure, learn naked to follow the naked Christ by self-discipline. The lover of the Cross of Christ will seek to give and not to count the cost.

Now in practical everyday living, this call means:

1. An absolute givenness to God to know his will and to follow it. I have no will but his: 'Show me thy will, I am content to do it.' AM I? It is so easy to say.

2. An opening of our whole being to the action of the Holy Spirit, that he may work the work of transformation in us. Do we think often enough of the work of the Holy Spirit and the power of the sevenfold gifts that we received at our Confirmation?

3. Learning the disciplined life of love by putting first things first: curing some habit which makes us less able to give God the honour due unto his Name, such as a habit of going to bed late which makes us too tired to get up in the morning;

such habits can hold back the whole of our spiritual growth. Are we careful not to fall below the Christian standard in our human friendships, personal relationships or ideas of morality and truth generally?

4. Have we a growing horror for sin, our own first and then the world's? This horror for sin manifests itself in the spirit of compunction which grieves for sin because it is an insult to God's holiness. So often our sorrow is only because we have fallen below our own estimate of ourselves; or, a slightly higher motive, because we realize that our sin has hurt someone else. The real spirit of compunction sees sin in its relation to God, and only afterwards in relation to others or ourselves. Yet, let us remember that God does not despise lower motives—if we can't begin at the top of the ladder, let us, at least, put our feet on the lower rungs and mount steadily.

5. Have we a spirit of compassion which is a reflection of the Divine Compassion, for others' sins and for our own slow response to grace?

6. Do we manifest in our lives the spirit of divine charity, for love of man must go hand in hand with love of God? There is only one measure to judge how far the law of charity is operating: 'God so loved the world that he gave his only begotten Son', and, as St Bernard says, 'the measure of love is to love without measure'. We may be tempted to think that this is impracticable, but scripture leaves us in no doubt of the duty of the love of the brethren.

7. Do we make use of and accept what is called 'the sacrament of the unexpected'? Circumstances, even if they are wrong, are allowed by the permissive will of God, and he has some message to teach us through them if we accept them as from him, as the meeting place of our love with his love.

8. Lastly, if reparation is to enter into the whole of life, we must use all things sacramentally, and recognize the divine underneath. Do we use all that God gives us in a spirit of sacrificial love, bringing his spirit into the soullessness of so much in the modern world where everything is done for man's material welfare while the life of the spirit is neglected?

16

Above all, growth in holiness means growth in the spirit of love. God is love, and if we are growing in union with the God of love, we must also be growing in union with one another— that is the meaning of the transverse of the vertical and the horizontal. It comes to this: Have ye the mind of Christ, of the Christ who dwells within each one of us? If you are a wholly committed Christian, if you are going forth with a sense of vocation to bear witness to the power of redeeming love, then you must see every contact of your life in the context of a vocation to the demands of charity. We cannot love all with our natural affections, or find a natural compatibility with every-one, but we can meet every contact on the supernatural level, and once we are prepared to sanctify all our relationships in Christ, we shall find that natural human incompatibility will disappear in a marvellous way.

If you are to be channels of the vast charity of God, put love in where love is not, cultivate friendliness and gaiety in your-selves for the glory of God, that others may come to you in their need, not because of your own self, but because you are showing forth the spirit of God. If you are conscious of any failure in charity, and we are all frail and do fail at times, then do not let the seed of discord develop, but go at once and acknowledge to the person concerned that you have been lacking in love. One bitter person, one unkind tongue, can work havoc in a parish, sow discord among a school staff, and suspicion between husband and wife.

Lack of charity is fodder on which the Enemy can feed and use in engendering disunity, and it will cut across the reality and truth of our sharing in our Lord's overcoming. Let us put love in where love is not. There is that saying of St John of the Cross, 'At eventide they will examine thee in love.' When, at the Last Day we stand before our Lord, we shall be judged not by worldly standards of efficiency and popularity, but by our showing forth the spirit of love by which we shall have helped to heal the wounds of the world, or, alas, have failed to do so and so added to the distortion.

The spirit of love is the basic principle of the Christian

response, and it must be safeguarded and strengthened by our union with our Lord. The life of charity is fostered and maintained also by the disciplined mind, will and affections—which brings us to the subject of the kinds of discipline which are basic to our growth in holiness and development in the life of prayer.

We are all aware of the growing restlessness of the world, which is now reaching a terrible stage; and most of us are also conscious of that same restlessness in our own minds, especially during prayer time. Modern life is hurried, and many feel they need something which is constantly varied and changing to hold their interest. That is what is meant by 'the spirit of the world'. We are thinking of the world which has lost its hold on the Christian faith and has therefore has lost its true centre. Minds which should be ministering to the eternal order are preoccupied with things of passing worth. We must fight this with a *disciplined mind*. Therefore, on behalf of the world, as well as for the order of your own souls, lay this deeply to heart:

1. Be aware, and use self-discipline as to the subjects upon which you allow your minds to dwell.

2. Concentrate, think things out, ponder deeply. Do not flit from one subject to another. Lack of direction and idle dreaming can be a habit which fosters self-absorption and pride.

3. Curb vagaries; have done with futile imaginations and day dreams; above all, do not spend your thoughts going over old grievances, whether they be real or not.

How can an undisciplined mind be an instrument for the mind of God? Such a mind, given to vanities, becomes prey to illusions and to fantastic distortions of the truth. To combat this we must develop a mind well stored, disciplined and able to learn wherever true learning may be found. Such a mind becomes, thank God, the medium for the Holy Spirit's work. But the Spirit cannot lead undisciplined minds. What can a secularized world know of the Word of God—and that is true also of the soul.

Given a disciplined mind, the Holy Spirit will take possession and will illuminate it as he alone can, and make it more and more sensitive to the light of divine truth. Hardly perceptible is

18

the Spirit's touch except by those who have gained this radiant simplicity, but the Spirit leads always from complexity to unity, and on to that loving gaze by which we are kept in God.

The will must make its choice and decision on those things which the mind presents. Here in the *discipline of the will* lies the secret of true self-command and ability to respond to the prompting of the Holy Spirit. The first step needed in making a choice is a decision in any given instance as to what is right in itself, apart from all self-interest and the subtle influences which our past wanderings have created or present circumstances conjoined. We must press through these influences at any given moment, and work to identify our will with the holy will of God. There are three stages in this identification:

1. To *do* God's will and overcome all reluctance.
2. To *love* God's will, when the soul counts it all joy to suffer.
3. To *will* God's will, which is the path of the saints as they fill up what is behind of the suffering of Christ for his body's sake, and that is the way of sanctity.

Much prayer is needed and a humble spirit to attain to the soul's true end in God. It is the will redeemed by Christ and the affections ordered by him that will abide in his love. It is all of the love of God, all centred in God, and all radiating out from God.

A HIDDEN LIFE

So the circle is now complete and we can go back to our starting point. A consideration of the practice of the discipline I have described brings us back to the place where we learn this work—in matters great and small—and a recognition of the importance of the offering of our daily lives wherever God has placed us. It may mean that some of you will want to re-organize your lives in the light of some of the matters we have discussed. But for many of you the message is to return to the daily round, the common task, in deeper penitence and dependency on God.

I hope you will go forth from this weekend with a greater understanding of your vocation and its relation to the work of the community and the Church. We want to achieve perfection so quickly, but we must be patient with our own slow growth and take encouragement from the fact that we are all members of the body of Christ: the Fellowship is one with the community, the community is part of the one Church on earth which is part of the Corpus Domini, the whole mystical body, and patience and fortitude are among the fruits of this membership. As the years go by, we hardly perceive any change in ourselves, yet the hidden work of the Holy Spirit goes on to recreate and to perfect in us the image of God which has been revealed to us in the face of Jesus Christ.

A life of reparation demands great purity of heart, and a life of hiddenness in God, but it is not self achievement in giving self, but in being sanctified in losing self. It is a life within the Church for the sake of the Church. As Father Gilbert Shaw reminds us:

> In the end of an age the garment of the past can no longer be patched into new clothes: it has to be unwoven in order to be rewoven, and in order that it should be rewoven, the loom must first be set up. That setting up of the loom is the first task. Those called for that will not have the seeing of the pattern of the new way, only the discipline and making sure that the framework is not what they imagine but what God gives them to construct. In a day when so many either seek to patch or to weave bits of cloth of old patterns, it is hard to be occupied with the framework of the loom, but without it there can be no new weaving to bring in, not a patched, but a resurrection garment.

The old order is changing, yielding place to new. We here may not live to see the new pattern of the cloth, but the contemplative life and contemplative prayer are of God and stand for the eternal values which the world cannot destroy or distort. Every contemplative, whether in the cloister or in the world, is a living witness to the truth of God that is unshakeable.

In the days of crisis, or at a time as at present when the temporal scene is shifting, the Christian's faith and love must be nothing less than a message of the unity of love as revealed by the triumphant Passion of Christ. The falsity of the statement that a mere belief in Christ is an adequate protection against chaos will be found wanting; the truth is that Christ is *in* the chaos redeeming the world to himself, and in our work of reparation we are alongside the Redeemer in the chaos, so we too have to go right down into it.

But we are not alone: through the blood of his martyrs, the integrity of his confessors, and the prayers of his saints, God draws the world to himself. They are the witnesses of those things which are unshakeable. It is their prayer that is gathered into the eternal worship of heaven, and returns into the earthly disorder with the divine power of love as the judgment on those things which pass away. We can look up and take comfort that as members of the mystical body we have fellowship with the saints. We draw upon their fuller participation in the energy and unity of love as they, with our great High Priest, by their prayers surround and support us, sustaining our weak efforts of prayer and witness.

The risen Christ brings to his Church the fruits of his Passion which are peace and joy, and the reflection of these gifts will be seen on the faces of those who have heard the voice of God and felt the attraction of his love. So, therefore, let your light, his light in you, so shine before men that they may glorify your Father which is in heaven.

O God, our heavenly Father, who by thy blessed Son Jesus Christ hast declared thy Name unto us, that the love wherewith thou has loved him may be in us and he in us, graciously behold thy servants, and so enable us by thy Holy Spirit, that in obedience to our vocation, we may ever yield ourselves to thee as an offering of adoring, contrite love, that so thou mayest fully accomplish in us the good pleasure of thy will for others and for ourselves to the glory of thy holy Name, who with the same thy co-eternal Son and Holy Spirit art one God, world without end. Amen.

Suggestions for Further Reading

Angela Ashwin: *Heaven in Ordinary*, Mayhew McCrimmon, 1985.

Maria Boulding: *Marked for Life*, SPCK, 1979.

Dom John Chapman: *Spiritual Letters*, Sheed and Ward, 1935.

John Dalrymple: *Letting Go in Love*, DLT, 1986.

Gonville ffrench-Beytagh: *A Glimpse of Glory*, DLT 1986.

Austin Farrer: *Lord I Believe*, Faith Press, 1958. *The Triple Victory*, Faith Press, 1965. *The One Genius*, readings through the year with Farrer, selected by Richard Harries, SPCK, 1987.

F.P. Harton: *The Elements of the Spiritual Life*, SPCK, 1932.

André Louf: *Teach Us to Pray*, DLT, 1974.

Robert Llewelyn: *Prayer and Contemplation*, SLG Press, 1975. *With Pity not with Blame*, DLT, 1982. The 'Enfolded in Love' series, Robert Llewelyn, Gen. Ed., daily readings, each book using an author such as Julian of Norwich, de Caussade, St Teresa, DLT, 1980–.

Thomas Merton: *New Seeds of Contemplation*, Burns and Oates, 1961. *The Climate of Monastic Prayer*, Irish Univ. Press, 1969.

Eric Mascall: *The Secularization of Christianity*, DLT, 1965. *Jesus, Who He Is and How We Know Him*, DLT, 1985.

Donald Nicholl: *Holiness*, DLT, 1981.

A.M. Ramsey: *The Glory of God and the Transfiguration of Christ*, Longmans, 1949. *The Gospel and the Catholic Church*, Longmans, 1936. *Be Still and Know*, Fount, 1982.

Archimandrite Sofrony: *The Undistorted Image*, Faith Press, 1958.

L.S. Thornton: *Common Life in the Body of Christ*, Dacre Press, 1941.

Esther de Waal: *Seeking God*, Collins, 1984.

Rowan Williams: *The Wound of Knowledge*, DLT, 1977.

W.H. Vanstone: *The Stature of Waiting*, DLT, 1982.